D0516105

ISLAND OF LIGHT

PHOTOGRAPHS BY

Robert Cooper

AN ILLUSTRATED COLLECTION OF PRAYERS

David Adam

HENDRICKSON PUBLISHERS

Hendrickson Publishers, Inc.
P. O. Box 3473
Peabody, Massachusetts 01961 - 3473

ISBN 1-56563-767-4

First published in Great Britain in 2002 by
Society for Promoting Christian Knowledge
Holy Trinity Church
Marylebone Road
London NW1 4DU

Designed and produced by Mary Gorton
Printed in Denmark by Nørhaven Book

Hendrickson Publishers' edition reprinted by arrangement
with Society for Promoting Christian Knowledge.

Hendrickson Edition First Printing – 2002

FOREWORD

A statue of Saint Aidan in Holy Island churchyard has him holding a flaming torch, a symbol of the light flowing out from the Island to Northumbria, to the nation and beyond. The light of the early island saints such as Aidan, Cuthbert, Cedd and Chad has attracted pilgrims to the Island since the seventh century. When the Vikings made their first raid on Britain, it was on Holy Island, and the Scholar Alcuin from the court of Charlemagne wrote, 'The holiest place in Britain is given a prey to pagan people.' In Alcuin's day it was the main place of pilgrimage in England and esteemed of great holiness and saintly light.

The light of the early saints and the holiness of the Island still attracts pilgrims and seekers in their thousands each year. Groups walk across the sands in their bare feet; others come carrying large pilgrim crosses for the Good Friday and Easter ceremonies. Some come for learning, or just to be in this special place and let the light of the saints influence their lives.

The Island is also an amazing place for natural light, as many of the photographs by Robert Cooper reveal. There is a quality of light around the Island that is very special. As a small island surrounded by sea, it gains from reflected light off the water. To the west of the Island, if the tide is out when the sun sets, all the pools and the meandering streams pick up the glow from the sky, making intricate and ever changing patterns of light and shadow of a wonderful radiance. It is one of the few places in our land where you can see the sun rise and set in the sea without having to travel. It is truly an Island of light.

DAVID ADAM

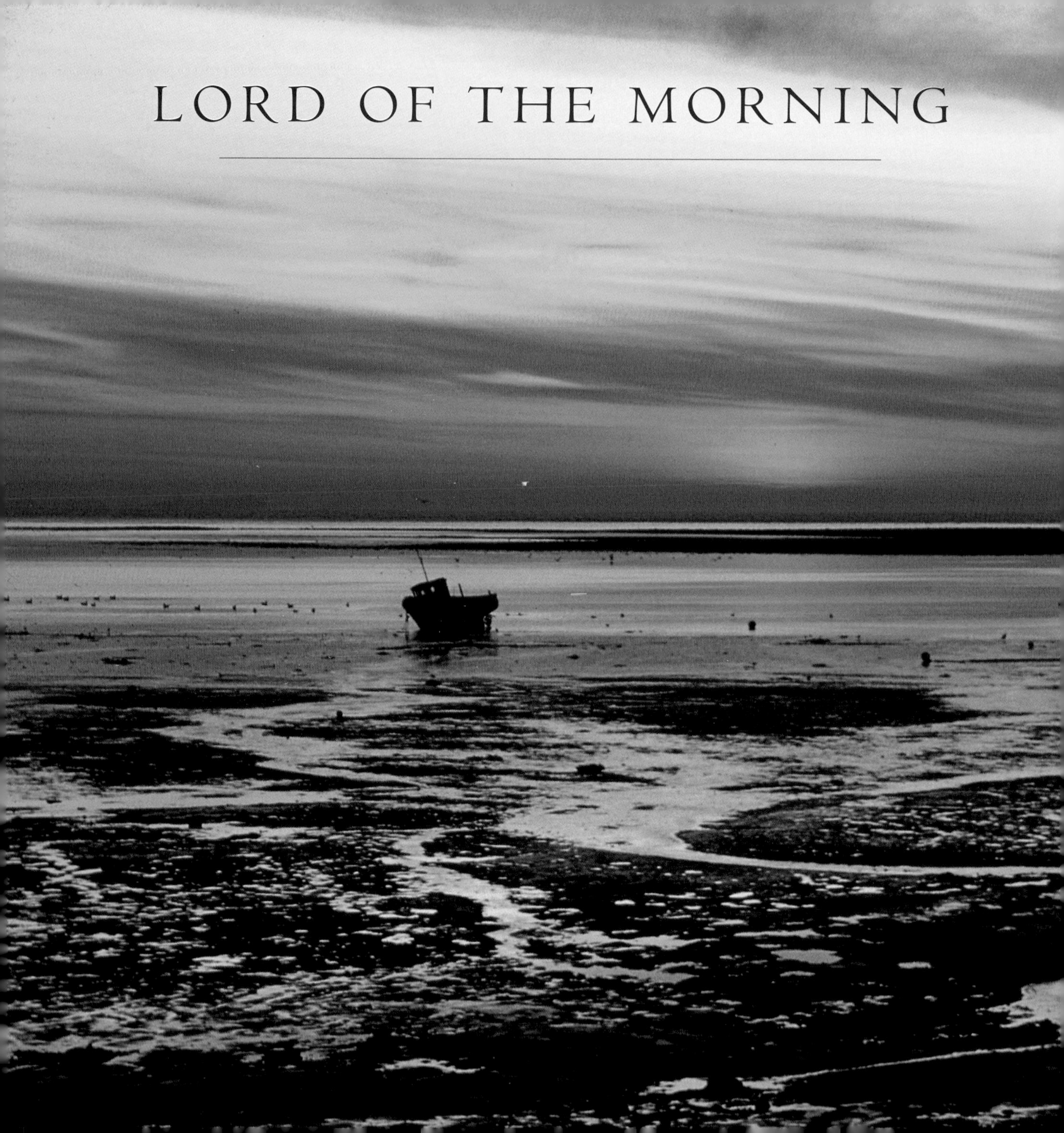

LORD OF THE MORNING

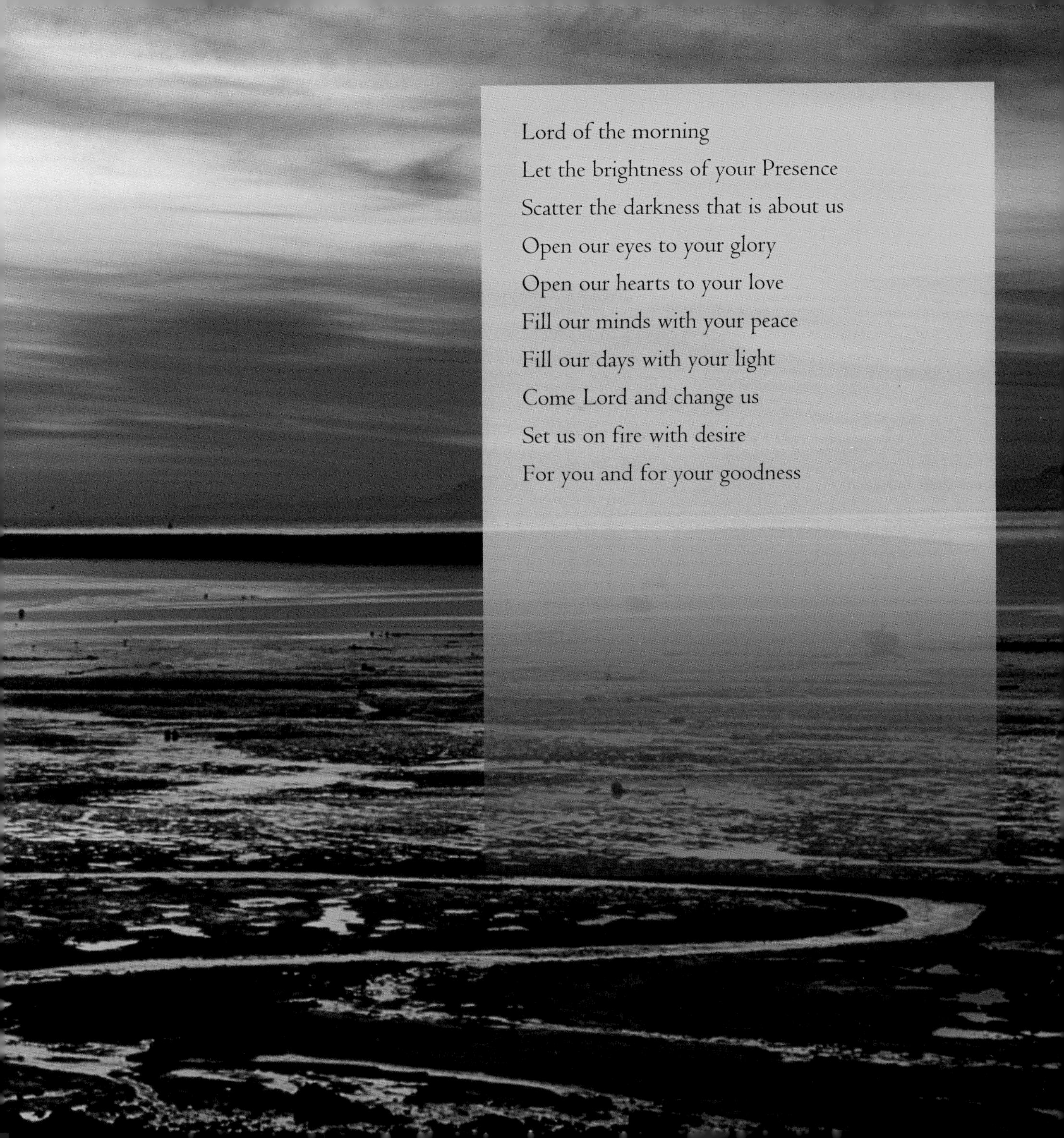

Lord of the morning
Let the brightness of your Presence
Scatter the darkness that is about us
Open our eyes to your glory
Open our hearts to your love
Fill our minds with your peace
Fill our days with your light
Come Lord and change us
Set us on fire with desire
For you and for your goodness

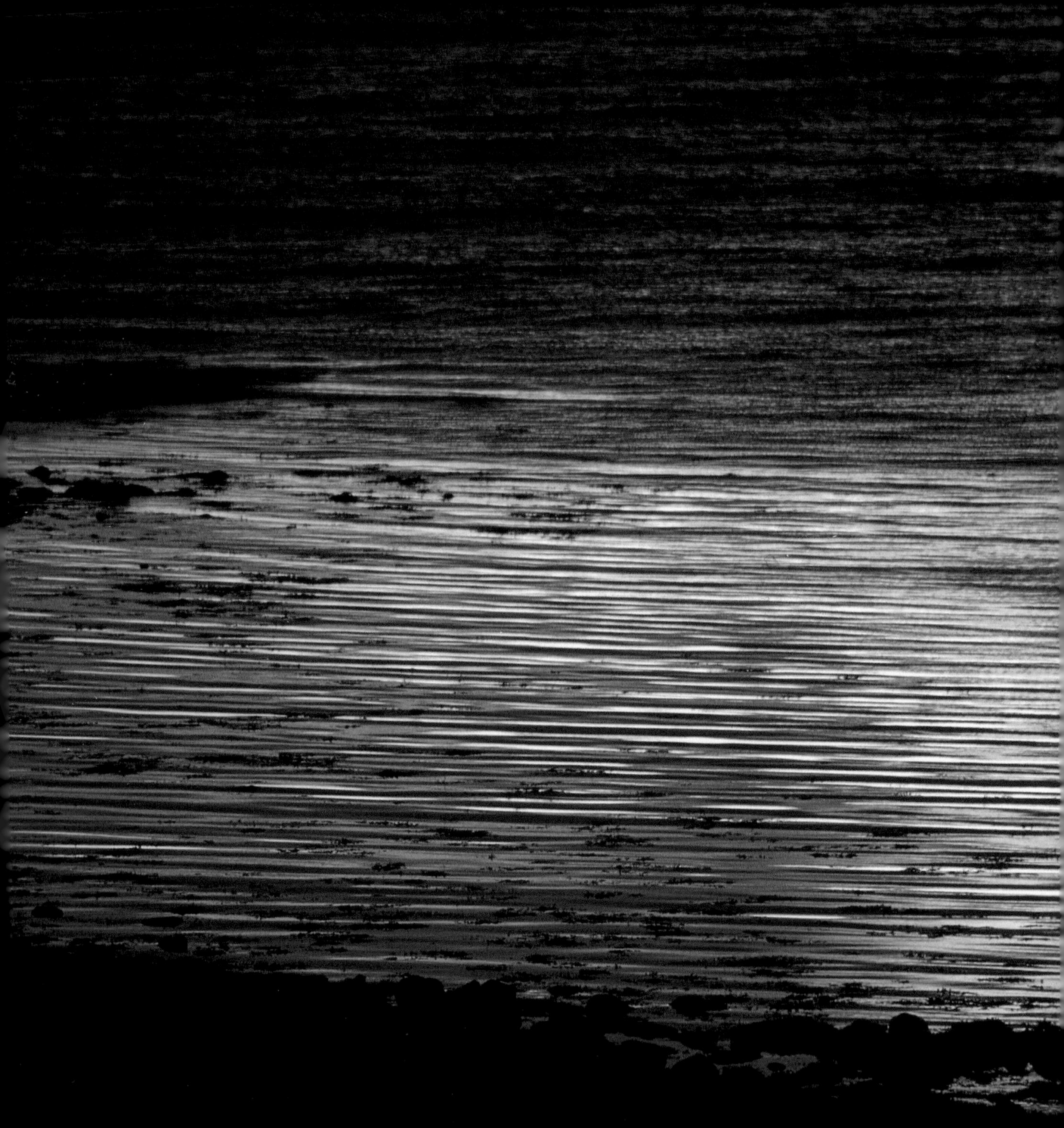

JESUS MY PROTECTOR

Jesus
Mary's Son
Holy One
My shield
My protector
My strong tower
My encircler
Keep me in your sight
Protect me this day
And through the night
Protect me this day
And through the night

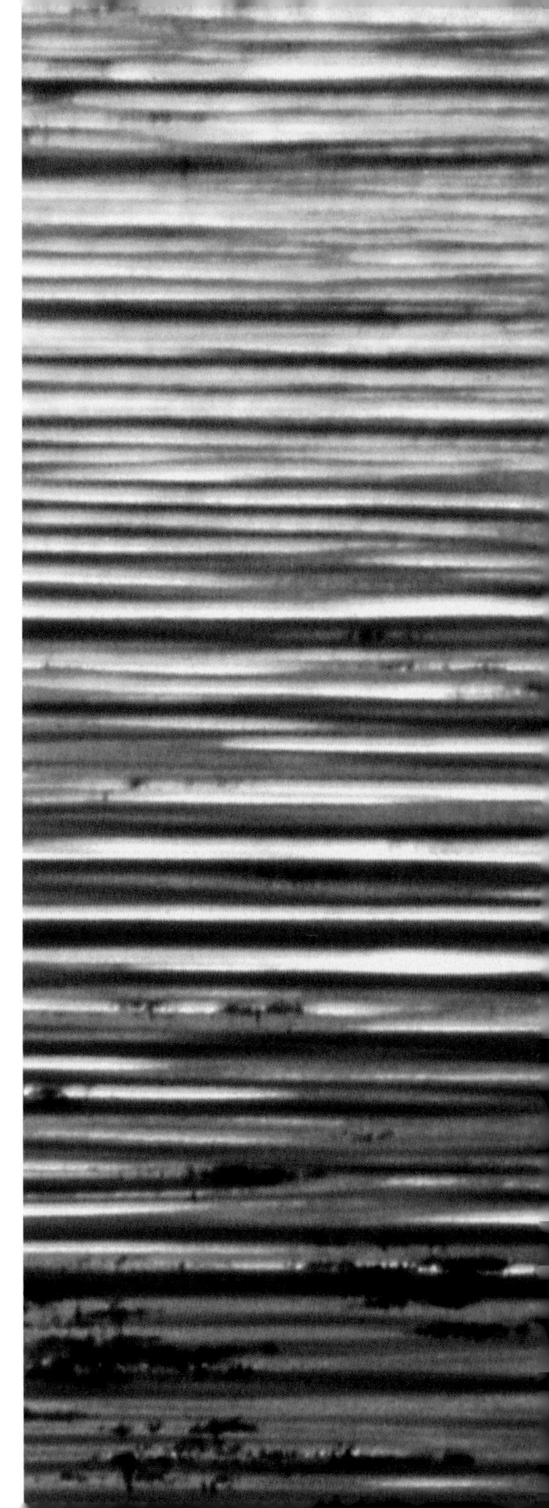

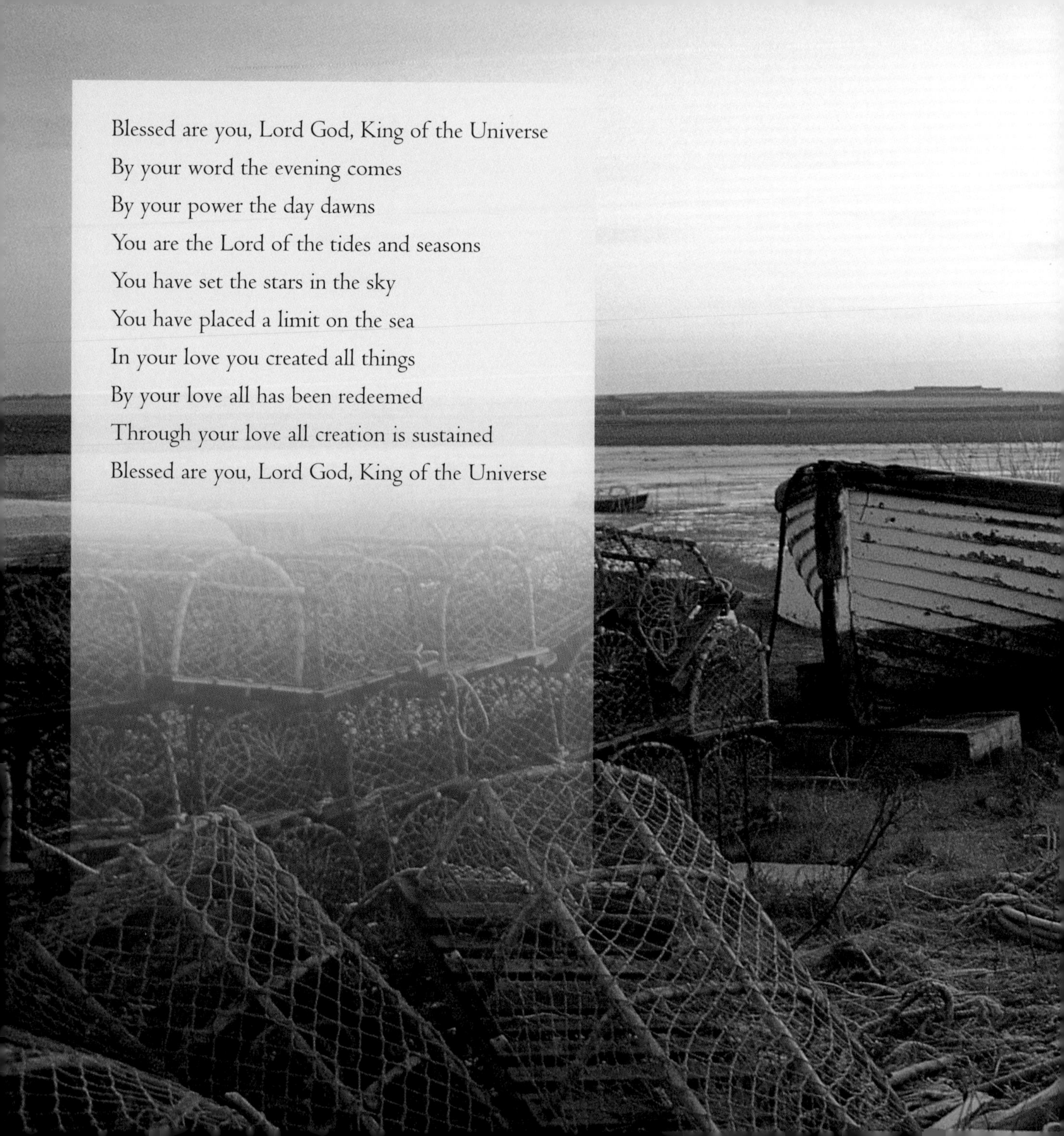

Blessed are you, Lord God, King of the Universe
By your word the evening comes
By your power the day dawns
You are the Lord of the tides and seasons
You have set the stars in the sky
You have placed a limit on the sea
In your love you created all things
By your love all has been redeemed
Through your love all creation is sustained
Blessed are you, Lord God, King of the Universe

DIVINE PRAISES

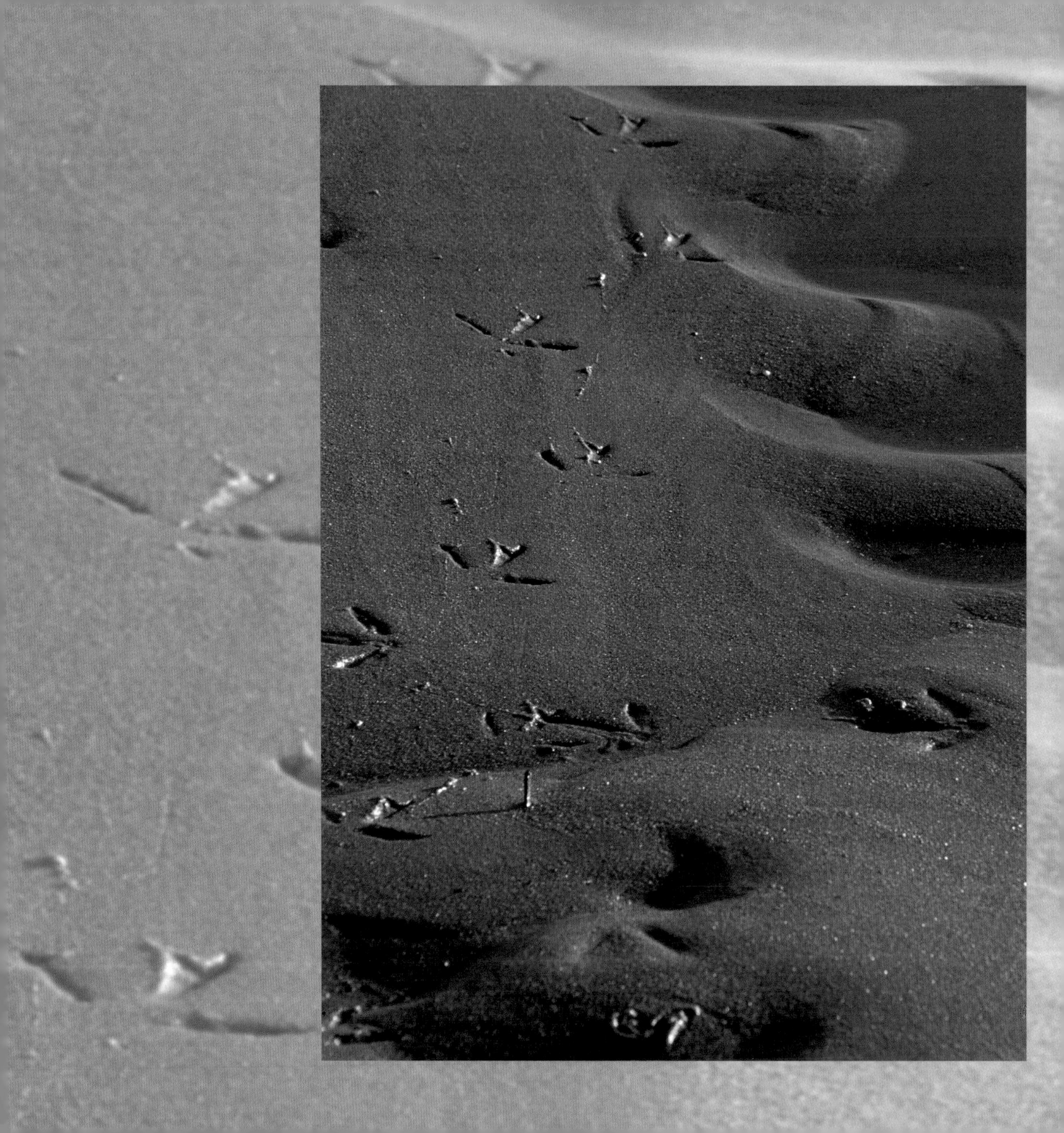

THE MYSTERY OF GOD

God is deeper than the ocean
More mysterious than the sea
The more I plunge into your depths
Greater treasures do I find
The more I find the more I seek
I rejoice in your depths
I long to know your mysteries
I am immersed in your presence
Grant that I may reveal your love
And come to you in adoration and awe

LORD OF LAND AND SEA

Lord of land and sea
Reveal your self to me
Keep my vision clear
To know you are near
At the rising of the dawn
In the freshness of the morn
In the raging of the sea
In the birds' sweet harmony
In each star set in the sky
In all places dark and deep
In the mountains high and steep
In every place and every coast
Father, Son and Holy Ghost
Keep my vision clear
To know you are near
Lord of land and sea
Reveal your self to me

THE SHELTER OF GOD

Lord you are my hiding place
A shelter from the storm
A protection from the heat
I rest under the cover of your wing
Your love is all around me
Above me to uplift me
Beneath me to support me
Behind me to protect me
Before me to guide me
Around me to shield me
Within me to strengthen me
Lord you are my hiding place
This day and forever
This day and forever

GOD OF THE DEEP

God of the deep
Pour your eternity into our hearts
For we hunger and thirst for you
We seek to know that we live in you
And that you make your home with us
Drive from us doubt and darkness
Dispel all our despair and distress
That in your light we may rejoice
Free us from fear and fretfulness
Expel our anxiety and anxiousness
That in your peace we may find rest
Amid the storm and the tempest
When the elements rage and roar
Give us the faith to stand firm
To be still in your power and love

GOD WITH US

God our beginning
God our goal
God our journey
God in our soul

God our pathway
God our light
God our guidance
God our might

God our yearning
God our friend
God our hope
God at the end

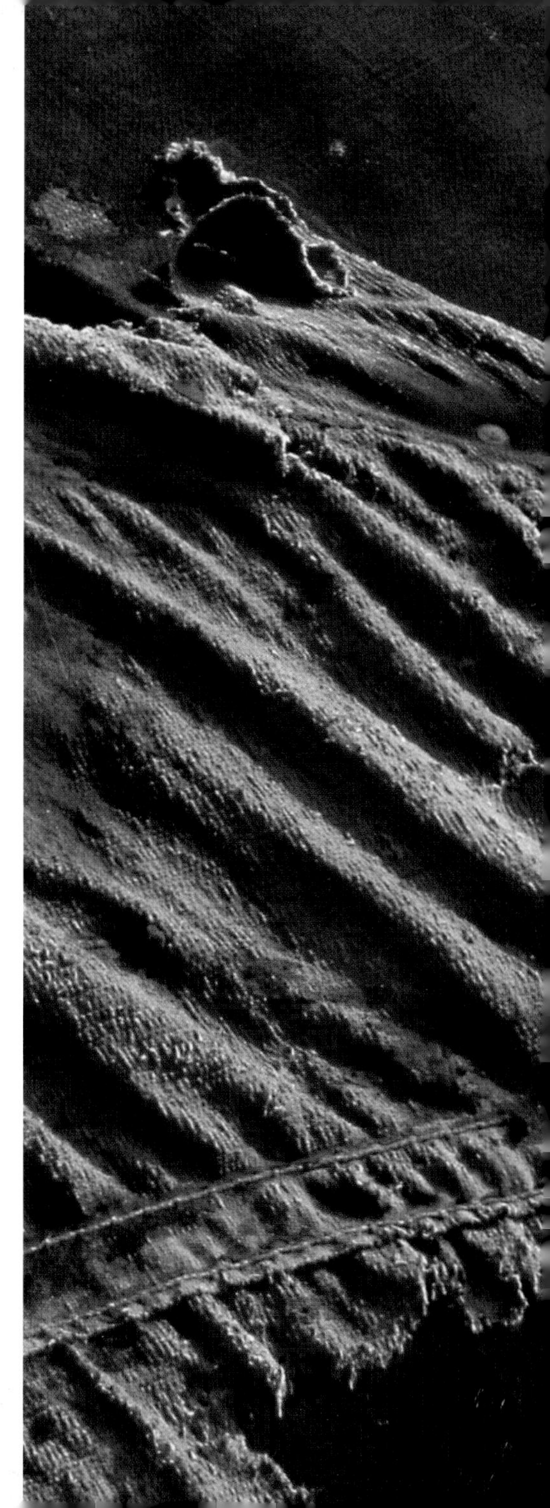

BLESS THIS PLACE

Loving Lord
Bless this place
Let your love be here
Fill it with your peace
Let your joy be here
Fill it with your grace
Let your light be here
Fill it with your power
Let us know you are here
Fill us with your presence

ALWAYS THERE

God above us
God about us
God beneath us
God within us
When we lose our grip
Keep your hold on us
When we stumble and fall
Uplift and support us
When our faith wavers
Dear Lord keep faith with us
When our vision is dimmed
In love, Lord, look upon us
In our darkest hour
Lord let your light surround us
When far away we wander
You are never far from us
God above us
God about us
God beneath us
God within us

SANCTUARY

We come to your sanctuary
To sit in silence
In singleness of heart
To seek you
In sureness of spirit
To serve you

Saviour, supply our needs
Still our hearts
Satisfy our spirits
That we may surrender our souls
And be strengthened by you

WIDE HORIZONS

Good and gracious God
Grant to our eyes wide horizons
Increase our vision to see
Beyond the obvious and into the depths
Let us walk ways that are new
Where we do not know the destination
Let us journey in joy and in hope
Among so many troubles and dangers
Surround us with your protection and peace
May we know that heaven and earth are one
That nothing separates us from you
And your abiding love in Christ Jesus

REFLECTED LIGHT

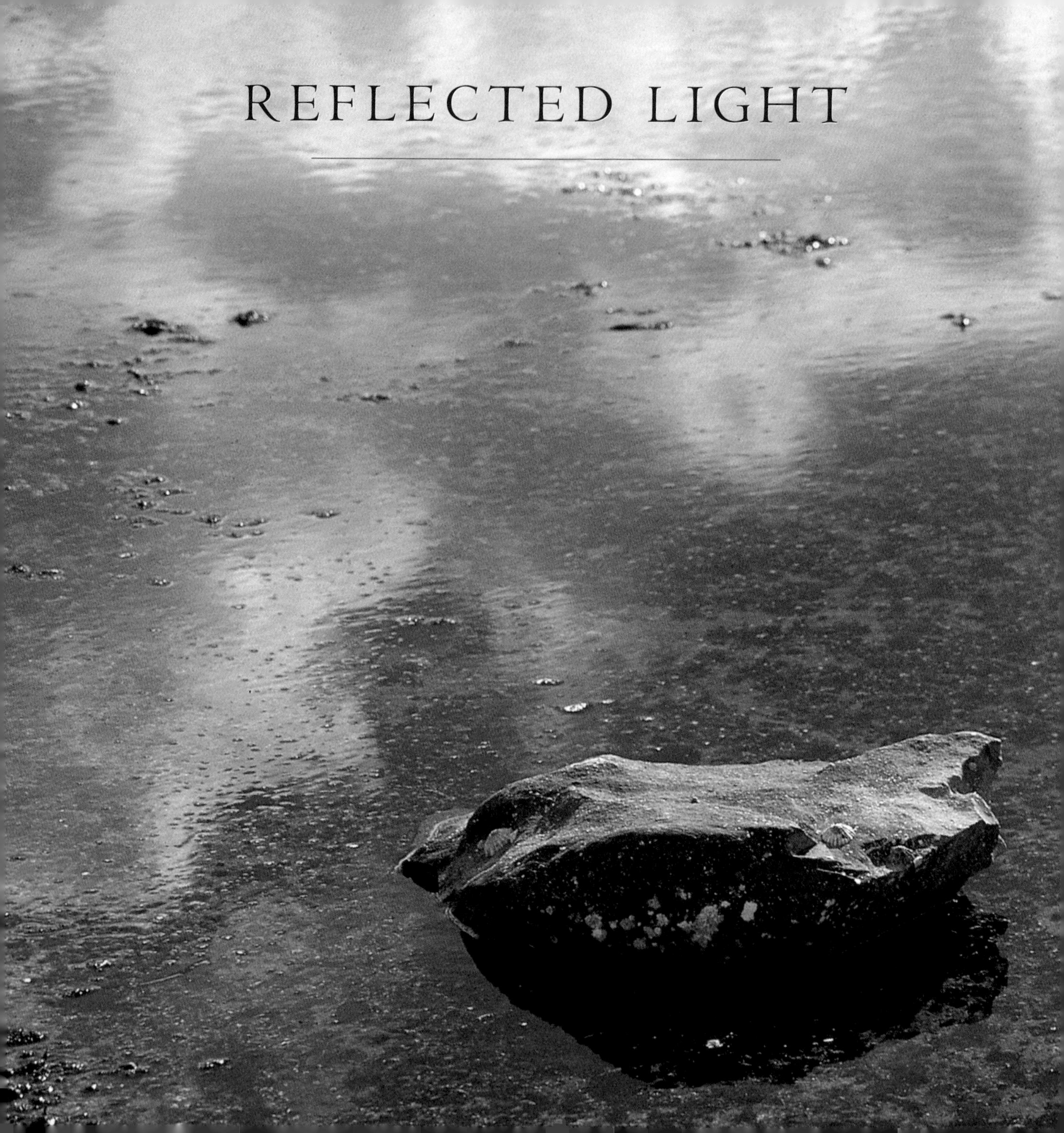

As the darkened pool is stilled
It reflects the blue sky above
So may my quiet mind reflect
O God, your glory and your love

As the sea glows in the moonlight
Light of lights, come and shine
Let my life reveal your light
Until I reflect the light divine

As the earth reflects the sunshine
Light of the Creator be mine
Light of the Saviour be mine
Light of the Spirit be mine

Each dawning and each night
O God, may I reflect your light
Each night and each day
Light of God, guide my way

AWARENESS

God give me your love
Give me your joy
Give me your peace
That I may live life to the full
And in awareness of you

God give me your guidance
Give me your protection
Give me your power
That I may travel in hope
And in awareness of you

God give me your aid
Give me your strength
Give me your presence
That I may grow in faith
And in awareness of you

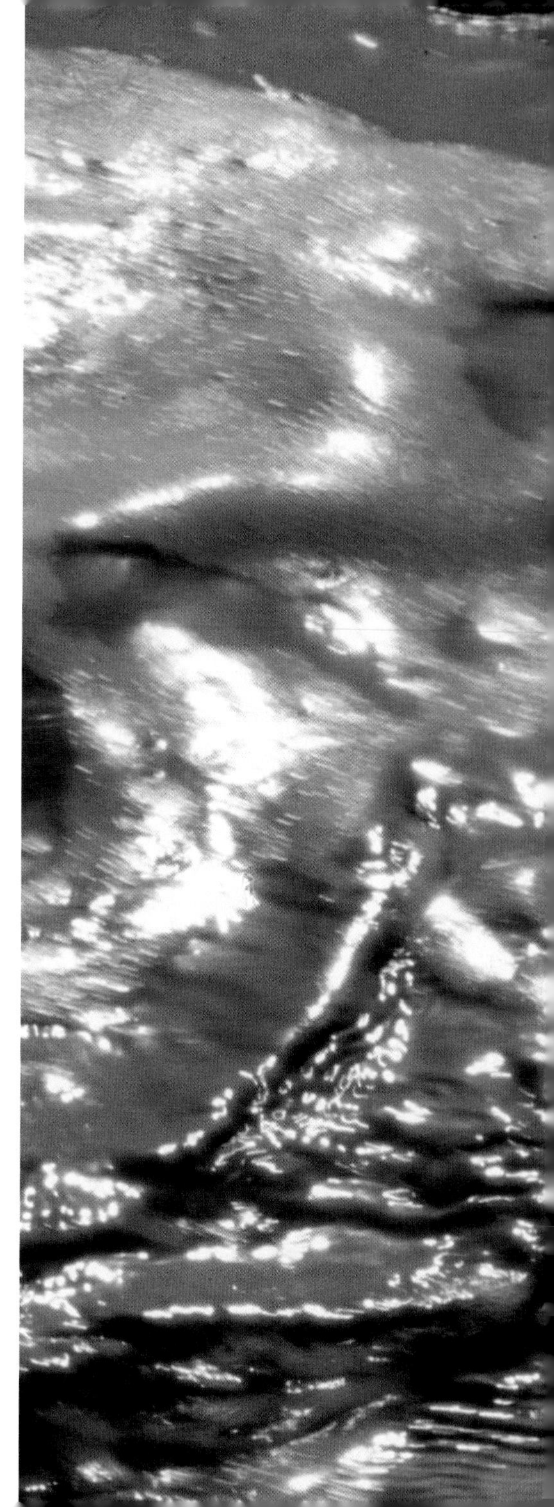

IN EVERY PLACE

Holy and loving God
There is no place you do not dwell
And every place where you are is holy
There is no creature that lacks your presence
And every creature through you is holy
In all things and in every place
Grant us vision to see you
Minds to seek you
Hearts to love you
Though poor our dwelling
You are with us and in us
You come to us and abide with us
You transform our poverty
By the glory of your presence

YOUR KINGDOM COME

In the stillness of this morning
In the day that is newly dawning
O Lord, your kingdom come

In your Church, in our singing
In our prayers we are bringing
O Lord, your kingdom come

Into a world that cries for peace
To the earth that wars may cease
O Lord, your kingdom come

Into our hearts and our wills
To our lives which the Spirit fills
O Lord, your kingdom come

To the lonely and the sad
To the tortured and driven mad
O Lord, your kingdom come

To all who have lost hope today
To all who are too ill to pray
O Lord, your kingdom come

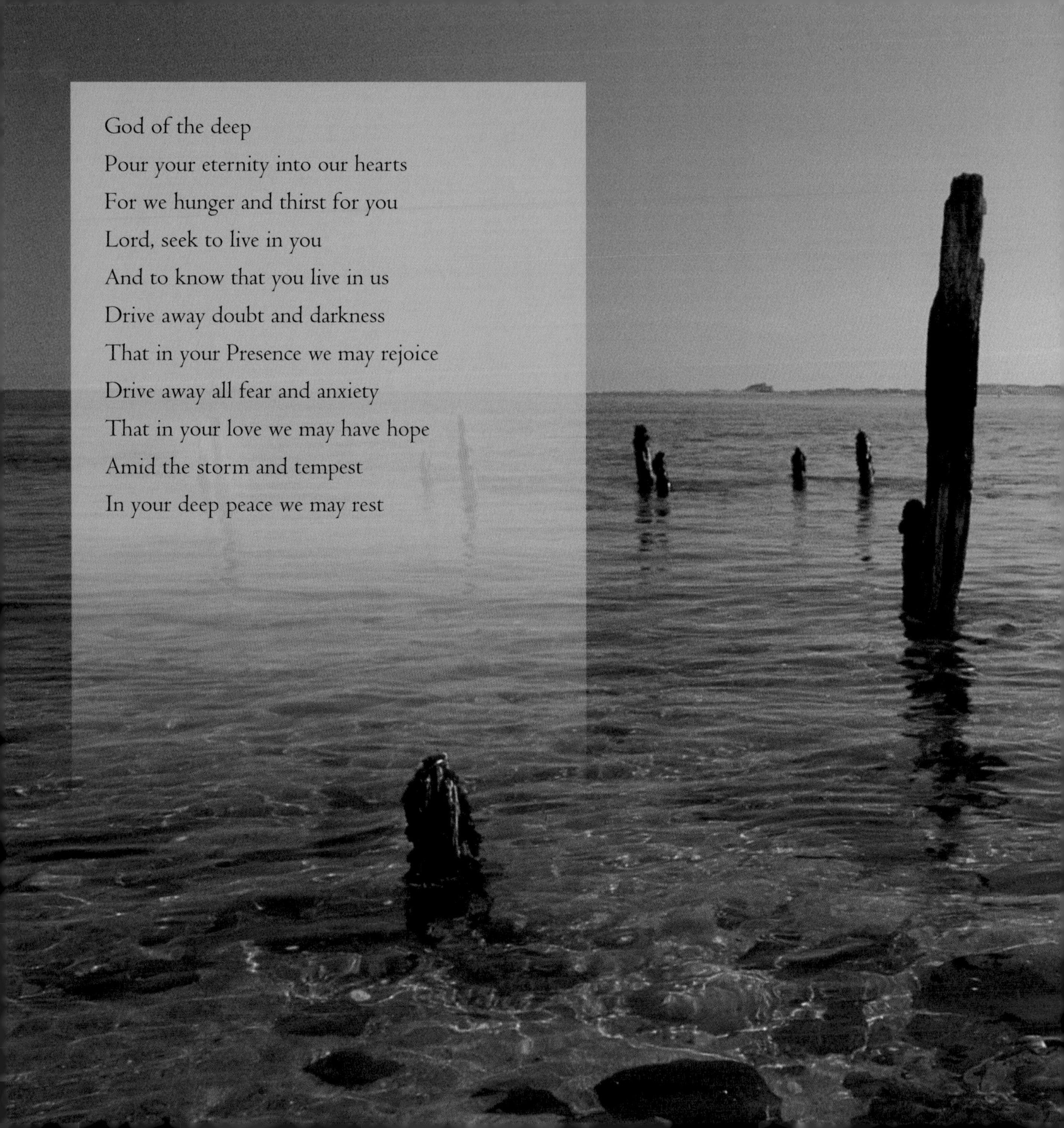

God of the deep
Pour your eternity into our hearts
For we hunger and thirst for you
Lord, seek to live in you
And to know that you live in us
Drive away doubt and darkness
That in your Presence we may rejoice
Drive away all fear and anxiety
That in your love we may have hope
Amid the storm and tempest
In your deep peace we may rest

FILL US LORD

GOD IN ALL

Lord let us know your presence
Your power in every living thing
In all creatures may we perceive you
That your great glory may be seen
Glory in every sunrise and the cloud
Glory in the seaweed and the sand
Glory in the waves' roar and the quiet
Glory in the stars and in the moon
Glory in the meeting of friends
Glory in the encounter with a stranger
Glory in our homes and in our loved ones
Glory in each journey and arrival
Glory in our being and in ourselves
Your glory in all of your creation
For you Lord fill your universe
Glory, glory, O Lord to you

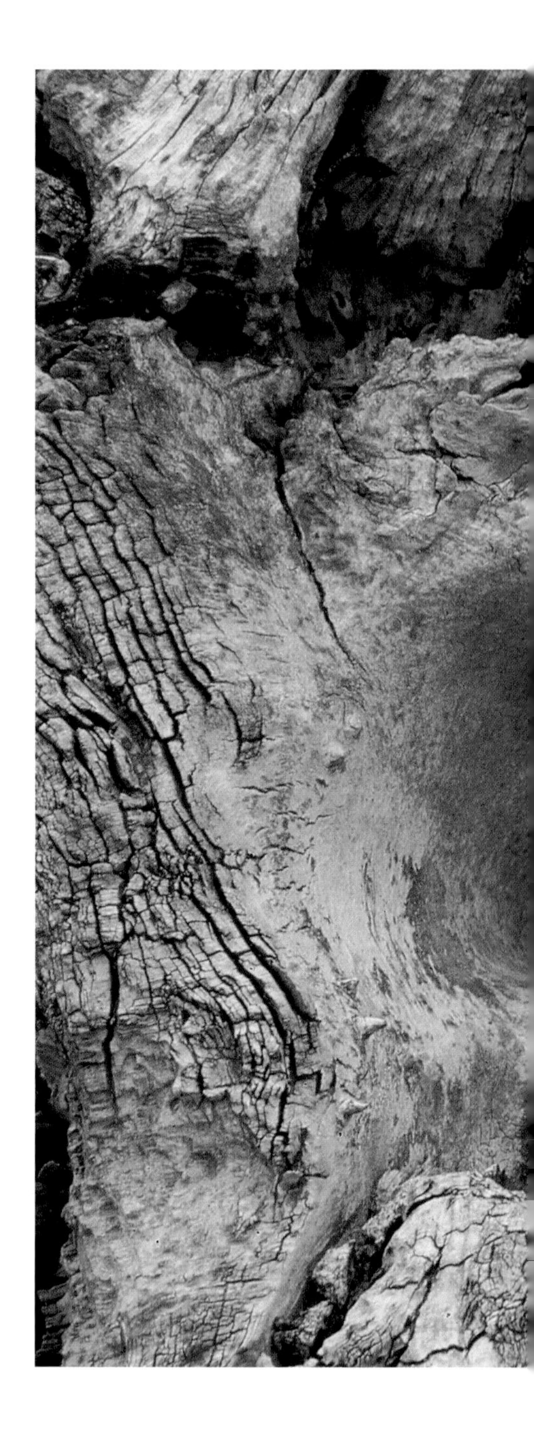

Prince of the universe
Master of the mysteries
Protect us in the dark hours
Until the morning light

Christ of the wounds
Christ of the glory
Grant us rest this night
Until the dawn breaks

Christ of the sorrows
Christ of great joy
Give us peace of mind
Now and forever more

NIGHT PRAYER

LORD OF LIGHT

Lord of light
Surround us with your brightness
Deliver us from the powers of darkness
In your light may we see light
The light of your grace
The light of your goodness
The light of your glory
Be about us and within us
That we may live as people of the light
People of the day and not of the darkness
Let your light guide us in our perplexities
Enlighten us in our sorrows
And surround us in our dangers
Lord of light, fill us with your light

ISLAND BLESSING

Bless, O Lord
This Island
This Holy Island
Make it a place
Of peace and joy
Make it a place
Of love and light
Make it a place
Of holiness and hospitality
Make it a place
Of grace and goodness
And begin with me

SEEING BENEATH THE SURFACE

'The sun is nice,' said Anna, 'but it lights things up so much that you can't see very far.'

I agreed that sometimes the sun was so dazzling that on occasion one was quite blinded. That wasn't what she meant.

'Your soul doesn't go very far in the daylight 'cos it stops where you can see... The night time is much better. It stretches your soul right out to the stars.'[1]

Anna's profound simplicity is enough to make anyone give up daylight photography! Everything we see is simply the effect of light reflected off surfaces, and Anna is right – there *is* a real temptation to dwell on the surface of things, 'to stop where you can see', especially if that surface appearance is beautiful. So how can we learn to see further and deeper? How can the eyes of our hearts be enlightened, as St Paul once put it?[2] The reflection in the photograph accompanying the prayer 'Reflected Light' offers us a visual clue. While everything that creates the image of the sky occurs in an infinitesimally thin layer on the surface of the pool, it is impossible to appreciate the reflection without allowing the eye to be drawn beneath the water's skin to where the clouds appear to be as deep under the surface as they are high in the sky. The way in which we use the word reflection to describe deep thought echoes this visual process of delving beneath the surface.

David Adam's prayers offer a model of this reflective process in action. It is our hope that this combination of words and pictures will draw readers into reflections of their own, and to experience what it means for their souls to be stretched right out to the stars. As the poet Rilke puts it:

Work of sight is done.
Now do heart work
On the pictures within you.

ROBERT COOPER

[1] Fynn, *Mr God, This is Anna,* Fount, 1979, p. 152 [2] Ephesians 1.18